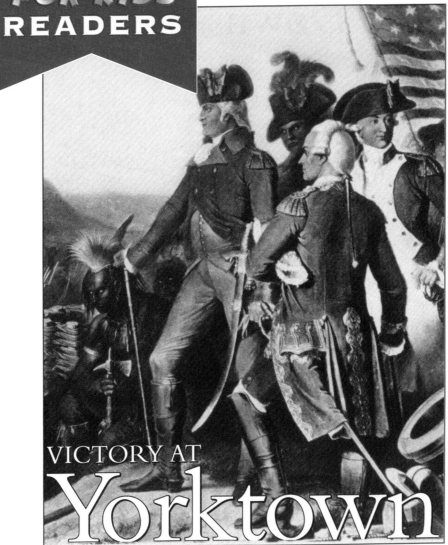

VICTORY AT
Yorktown

by Raymond P. Hill

Harcourt

Orlando   Austin   Chicago   New York   Toronto   London   San Diego

Visit *The Learning Site!*
www.harcourtschool.com

The World Turned Upside Down

O n the afternoon of October 19, 1781, more than 8,000 British and German troops paraded out of Yorktown, Virginia. Their flags, which normally would be flapping in the breeze, were wrapped in cloth cases. Shock and sadness marked the men's faces. Several of the marchers were in tears.

They were sad because they had just lost a battle. They were on their way to surrender to their enemies—American patriots and their French allies.

A British military band played a sad march as the men moved down a dirt road. The name of the march was "The World Turned Upside Down." None of the soldiers sang, although the tune did have words:

If ponies rode men and if grass ate cows,

And cats should be chased into holes by the mouse . . .

If summer were spring and the other way around,

Then all the world would be upside down.

The British and German soldiers had good reason to feel that their world had been turned upside down. About 3,620 British troops were at Yorktown, along with 1,665 Germans they had hired to fight with them, and several hundred Loyalists—American colonists who sided with Britain.

A major reason the British lost the Battle of Yorktown was the defeat of their fleet in nearby waters.

American and French troops were 17,600 strong and had outnumbered and outsmarted the British forces, cutting them off from fresh supplies for weeks. Hungry and sick, and with no way out, the British gave up.

The death toll showed which side had suffered more in the Battle of Yorktown. A total of 156 British, German, and Loyalist soldiers had died. The Americans had lost 20 soldiers. The French had lost 52.

The defeated troops were led by a red-coated British officer on horseback. He was Brigadier General Charles O'Hara, the second in command at Yorktown. The top British commander, Lieutenant General Charles Cornwallis, stayed behind. He said he was sick, but his sick feeling surely came from shame.

On a grassy plain General O'Hara came upon the 20,000 French and American troops. On one side of the road, French troops in white uniforms stood at attention. On the other side, American troops stood just as stiffly.

Most of the Americans wore the buff and blue uniforms of General George Washington's Continental Army. Other Americans wore either buckskins or homemade clothes of cotton or wool. Some were members of Virginia's militia, volunteers willing to risk their lives to defend their colony.

O'Hara halted his troops between the lines of French and American soldiers. On the American side, a tall man in buff and blue sat on a splendid white horse. That was General George Washington, the leader of the French and American troops. Near him, also on horseback, was the Marquis (mar•KEE) de Lafayette. Although French, Lafayette held the rank of major general in the Continental Army. He was just 24 years old.

Facing the Americans, the Comte de (Count of) Rochambeau (ROH•shahm•boh) sat on horseback in front of the French troops. Rochambeau, a lieutenant general, was the leader of French forces in North America.

Comte de Rochambeau

After 20 days of fighting, the British surrendered at Yorktown.

General O'Hara turned to Rochambeau and offered him Cornwallis's sword. The gesture was a traditional way of saying "I give up."

Rochambeau refused to accept the sword. He nodded toward the men across the road. "We serve the Americans," the French commander said. "General Washington will give you your orders."

O'Hara crossed the road and presented the sword to Washington. The American general accepted it politely.

Marquis de Lafayette

Given Name: Marie Joseph Paul Yves Roch Gilbert du Motier

Born: September 6, 1757, in France

Childhood: Born into a wealthy family. Orphaned at 12 years old. Joined the French army at 14. Married at 16 to a relative of the French king.

Military Career: Found the French army boring and left it. Joined the Continental Army as a major general in 1777, when he was 19. Served the American cause without pay. Paid his troops out of his own pocket. Distinguished himself in the battles of Brandywine and Yorktown.

Age at Yorktown: 24

Quote: "The Play, Sir, is Over." he wrote a friend after the British surrender.

After Yorktown: Tried to protect the French royal family in 1789, during the French Revolution. Forced into exile by the revolutionaries. Jailed in Austria. Returned to France in 1799.

Died: May 20, 1834 in Paris, France

Little-Known Fact: More than 400 buildings, parks, counties, and cities are named Lafayette or a version of Lafayette.

A Commander's Worries

Strong forts and warships allowed the British to control New York City.

Eight months earlier, in February 1781, the American Revolution was in its sixth year. Many Americans in all 13 colonies were growing tired of the conflict and the hardships that came with it. Continental Army soldiers were simply walking away from their posts and going home.

Washington's soldiers had little food, and they had not been paid for months. The Continental Congress, the breakaway colonies' government, had no money. To pay its bills, Congress relied on loans or contributions from the French.

One of Washington's fears was that the money from France was going to run out. He also worried that the French might pull out their troops. The French were helping him because they hoped to loosen Britain's grip on America. But now the French, too, seemed tired of the war.

General Henry Clinton

It was Washington's opinion that a victory over British forces in New York City would solve all these problems. New York was the headquarters of General Henry Clinton, Britain's top commander in America.

Many British warships were anchored in New York Harbor.

An American victory in New York would not only disrupt Britain's war plans, thought Washington, but it would also raise his soldiers' spirits. He was sure it would convince France that the Americans could win the war.

Washington knew that capturing New York wouldn't be easy. Forts ringed the city. More than 10,000 British soldiers guarded it. Washington had fewer than 4,000 troops in the area.

The French leader, Comte de Rochambeau, opposed an attack on New York. So did Admiral Louis de Barras. De Barras commanded France's naval forces in North America. In May 1781 Rochambeau proposed another plan. He suggested that American and French forces take on the British in Virginia. Rochambeau thought he could get some extra French warships to help. Washington had been born in Virginia. He had lived there all his life. He felt he could beat the British there if he had enough help.

Rochambeau wrote to the commander of a French fleet based in the French colony of Haiti. Rochambeau begged the admiral for ships, troops, and money.

George Washington

Given Name: George Washington

Born: February 22, 1732, in Virginia

Childhood: Son of a wealthy Virginia family. Studied math, literature, and land surveying. As a young man, worked as a surveyor.

Military Career: Officer in the Virginia militia during French and Indian War (1754–1763). Became the militia's top commander in 1755, at age 23. Appointed head of the Continental Army in 1775.

Age at Yorktown: 49

Quote: "We must take Cornwallis," he wrote Lafayette, "or be all dishonored."

After Yorktown: Presided over the 1787 Constitutional Convention, whose members wrote our nation's basic laws. Served two terms (1789–1797) as U.S. President. Retired to his Virginia plantation.

Died: December 14, 1799, at home

Little-Known Fact: Washington wore false teeth made of cows' teeth, human teeth, and elephant ivory—not wood.

Charles Cornwallis

Given Name: Charles Cornwallis

Born: December 31, 1738, in England

Childhood: Eldest son of a wealthy English family. Attended the University of Cambridge. Decided early to have a military career.

Military Career: Served in the Seven Years War (1756–1763). Opposed tax laws that triggered the American Revolution, yet agreed to fight in America. Captured Philadelphia, the American capital, in 1777. In 1780 took control of British forces in America's southern colonies.

Age at Yorktown: 42

Quote: "My situation now becomes very critical," he wrote General Henry Clinton just before his surrender.

After Yorktown: Served as governor of India in 1786–1793, and again in 1805. Served as governor of Ireland from 1798–1801.

Died: October 5, 1805, in Ghazipore, India

Little-Known Fact: The British had so much respect for Cornwallis that they never blamed him for losing the Battle of Yorktown.

Cornwallis Goes to Virginia

In 1781 Lieutenant General Charles Cornwallis commanded British troops in the southern colonies. He was stubborn and independent. Cornwallis didn't like taking orders from General Clinton in New York.

Cornwallis's American enemy in the South was Major General Nathanael Greene and his American troops. In March 1781 the two armies met head-on in North Carolina. This bloody battle cost Cornwallis 532 men, one-quarter of his force. But his veteran troops won the day, pushing Greene's army from the field. Greene moved his battered troops back to South Carolina.

Cornwallis, still in North Carolina, wondered if he should pursue Greene's force. He decided instead to move the war to Virginia.

Cornwallis marched into Virginia in May 1781, stopping along the way to pick up Americans loyal to Britain. His troops caused a lot of trouble there. They raided farms to steal food and horses. They looted and burned plantations. And they almost captured Thomas Jefferson, the author of the Declaration of Independence.

Lieutenant General Cornwallis was considered a brave leader during battle.

Even though Clinton was not happy about Cornwallis going into Virginia, he rushed 2,000 British and German soldiers there. Cornwallis now had more than 7,000 troops under his command. The Marquis de Lafayette was in Virginia, too, and he led fewer than 2,000 troops. He knew there was no way he could defeat Cornwallis with so few men.

In July, Clinton ordered Cornwallis to go to Virginia's southeastern coast. British warships needed a place to anchor safely. Cornwallis was told to set up a base for them.

Cornwallis moved his troops to the Yorktown peninsula on the Chesapeake Bay. The peninsula is 10 miles (16 km) across and 20 miles (32 km) long. North of it the York River flows into the bay. The James River flows along its southern edge. About 30 miles (48 km) from the peninsula's tip, the bay's mouth opens onto the Atlantic Ocean.

Yorktown was a peaceful little port on the York River. Fewer than 60 families lived there. Most of them had fled when Cornwallis's troops showed up in late July.

Yorktown seemed a perfect base for British ships. Since it was a port, it had docks, storehouses, and places to repair ships. It had an excellent location, too. The bay is about 200 miles (320 km) long. Its mouth is only 12 miles (19 km) across. By patrolling the bay's narrow entrance, British warships could easily control the whole bay. Troops at Yorktown could supply them with food and equipment.

In 1781 few British warships patrolled the Chesapeake area. But Cornwallis expected a British fleet to control the bay before summer ended.

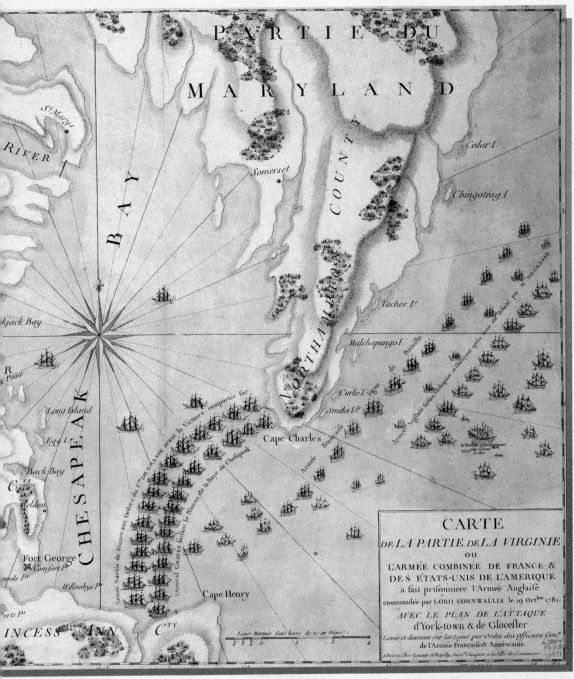

This French map shows the position of the troops at the Battle of Yorktown.

Admiral de Grasse

A large fleet did sail into the Chesapeake's waters on August 20, but the fleet was not the one Cornwallis expected. It was French Admiral de Grasse's entire fleet of 28 warships. His ships carried guns, ammunition, and more than 3,000 French soldiers. De Grasse turned the troops over to Lafayette, who was camped west of Yorktown at Williamsburg.

Sixteen days later a British fleet of 19 warships entered Chesapeake Bay. The French fleet pounced on them like hungry sharks. The ships exchanged cannon fire for 90 minutes. No ships were sunk, but many sailors on both sides were wounded or killed.

The battered British fleet fled back to its base in New York City. De Grasse's fleet now guarded the bay, completely cutting off escape for Cornwallis's army.

French ships fought off the British fleet in Chesapeake Bay.